THE LIFE
OF
MARY

EDITED BY INOS BIFFI
ILLUSTRATIONS BY FRANCO VIGNAZIA

LTP
LITURGY
TRAINING
PUBLICATIONS

GRACEWING

INDEX

INTRODUCTION

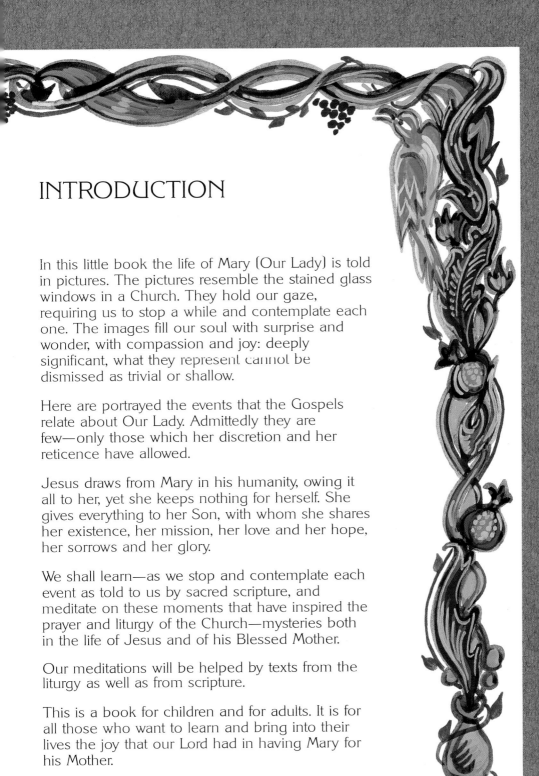

In this little book the life of Mary (Our Lady) is told in pictures. The pictures resemble the stained glass windows in a Church. They hold our gaze, requiring us to stop a while and contemplate each one. The images fill our soul with surprise and wonder, with compassion and joy: deeply significant, what they represent cannot be dismissed as trivial or shallow.

Here are portrayed the events that the Gospels relate about Our Lady. Admittedly they are few—only those which her discretion and her reticence have allowed.

Jesus draws from Mary in his humanity, owing it all to her, yet she keeps nothing for herself. She gives everything to her Son, with whom she shares her existence, her mission, her love and her hope, her sorrows and her glory.

We shall learn—as we stop and contemplate each event as told to us by sacred scripture, and meditate on these moments that have inspired the prayer and liturgy of the Church—mysteries both in the life of Jesus and of his Blessed Mother.

Our meditations will be helped by texts from the liturgy as well as from scripture.

This is a book for children and for adults. It is for all those who want to learn and bring into their lives the joy that our Lord had in having Mary for his Mother.

1
GOD SENDS AN ANGEL TO INVITE MARY

"The Virgin Mary, receiving
the angel's message in faith, conceived
by the power of the Spirit and bore
your Son in purest love.

TO BECOME THE MOTHER OF JESUS
(The Annunciation)

Your promise to Israel came
true, in Christ the hope
of all peoples was realised
beyond all expectation."

(from the Roman Liturgy)

2
MARY GOES TO HELP HER COUSIN ELIZABETH, WHO IS EXPECTING A BABY: WHO WILL BECOME FAMOUS

"Carrying God in her womb, the Virgin hastens to Elizabeth whose infant

JOHN THE BAPTIST, THE FIRST TO CALL JESUS THE LAMB OF GOD, THE SAVIOUR

(The Visitation)

immediately recognises Mary's
greeting with rejoicing . . ."

(from the Byzantine Liturgy)

3
JESUS IS BORN: JOSEPH IS WITH MARY WHOM HE HAD TAKEN AS HIS WIFE,

"So they went in haste and found Mary and Joseph, and the infant . . . . When they saw this, they made known the message that had been told them about this child. And all who heard it

AND THERE ARE
THE SHEPHERDS SENT
BY THE ANGELS
(The Nativity)

were amazed by what had been
told them by the shepherds.
And Mary kept all these things,
reflecting on them in her heart."

(from the Gospel of St. Luke)

4
MARY AND JOSEPH, AS IS THE CUSTOM, GO TO THE TEMPLE AND OFFER THEIR SON TO GOD, TAKING WITH THEM DOVES,

"The child's father and mother were amazed
at what was said about him;
and Simeon blessed them and said to Mary
his mother, 'Behold, this child

THE SYMBOLIC GIFT OF POOR PEOPLE, AND MEET THE ELDERLY SIMEON

(The Presentation in the Temple)

is destined for the fall and rise
of many in Israel, and to be a sign
that will be contradicted
(and you yourself a sword will pierce)'."

(from the Gospel of St. Luke)

13

5
MARY AND JOSEPH, IN ORDER TO SAVE JESUS FROM HEROD'S FURY,

"The angel of the Lord appeared to Joseph
in a dream and said, 'Rise, take
the child and his mother, flee to Egypt,
and stay there until I tell you.

HAVE TO TAKE HIM
TO A COUNTRY THAT
IS A LONG WAY OFF

(The flight into Egypt)

Herod is going to search for the child
to destroy him.' Joseph rose and took
the child and his mother
by night, and departed for Egypt."

(from the Gospel of St. Matthew)

15

6
JESUS, IN JERUSALEM, SEPARATES HIMSELF FROM HIS PARENTS, WHO FIND HIM AFTER THREE DAYS

"Mary, having anxiously sought her son, finds him occupied with his Father's affairs.

HAVING A DISCUSSION WITH THE DOCTORS IN THE TEMPLE

(The Loss and Finding of Jesus in the Temple)

The immaculate heart listens
to the infinite Word."

(A hymn to Mary by a contemporary author)

7
MARY ASKS JESUS TO HELP HER FRIENDS IN DIFFICULTY. THE WATER AT THE BANQUET

"There was a wedding in Cana in Galilee, and the mother of Jesus was there. Jesus and his disciples were also invited to the wedding. When the wine ran short, the mother of Jesus

IS MIRACULOUSLY CHANGED INTO WINE

(The Wedding at Cana)

said to him, 'They have no wine.'
And Jesus said to her, 'Woman, does
your concern affect me? My hour has
not yet come.' His mother said to
the servers, 'Do whatever he tells you.' "

(from the Gospel of St. John)

19

8
MARY, WITH
THE APOSTLE JOHN

"When Jesus saw his mother and
the disciple there whom he loved, he said
to his mother, 'Woman, behold, your son.'

AT THE FOOT OF THE CROSS
(The Crucifixion)

Then he said to the disciple, 'Behold,
your mother.' And from that hour
the disciple took her into his home."

(from the Gospel of St. John)

9
JESUS, AFTER HIS RESURRECTION AND HAVING SPENT

"May this loving mother, O Father, protect your people in their difficult pilgrimage

SOME TIME ON EARTH,
ASCENDED INTO HEAVEN
(The Ascension)

and support their steps on the rough way
as they await the return of the Master."

(from the Ambrosian Liturgy)

10
MARY AND THE APOSTLES RECEIVE THE HOLY SPIRIT

"O God, who gave the Holy Spirit
to the Apostles, who were assembled
in the Cenacle with Mary,
the mother of Jesus, grant us

THAT JESUS HAD PROMISED
(Pentecost)

through the intercession of
the Blessed Virgin the grace to preach
the gospel with the example
of the great work of your love."

(from the Roman Liturgy)

11
MARY LEAVES THIS EARTH. JESUS AWAITS THE SOUL OF HIS MOTHER

"Come dance, ye Christian bands
Ye faithful, clap your hands!
Come muster strong today,
Sing out! With loving heart
Bear every man his part!
For why in rich array,

AND WELCOMES HER, BODY AND SOUL, INTO HEAVEN

(The Assumption or Dormition)

Saint Mary, who gave birth
To God, doth quit this earth
For heav'n, to leave it never.
As Mother of that God,
Who once our planet trod,
Her we exalt for ever."

(from a hymn of the Eastern Church)

27

REFERENCES / ACKNOWLEDGEMENTS

Plate **1**: Solemnity of the Annunciation of the Lord. From the Preface of the Roman Liturgy.

Plate **2**: From the Akáthist hymn in honour of the Mother of God, Byzantine Liturgy.

Plate **3**: Lk. 2, 16–19.

Plate **4**: Lk. 2, 33–35.

Plate **5**: Mt. 2, 13–14.

Plate **6**: Hymn to Mary by a contemporary author.

Plate **7**: Jn. 2, 1–5.

Plate **8**: Jn. 19, 26–27.

Plate **9**: 'Memorial of Mary, Mother of the Church,' from a Preface of the Ambrosian Liturgy.

Plate **10**: From a collect of the Roman rite in honour of the Blessed Virgin Mary.

Plate **11**: *The Most Holy Mother of God in the songs of the Eastern Church translated from the Greek*, G. R. Woodward (Faith Press, 1919) no. 17, p. 27,

Apolytikion pro-eortion, at Vespers (Aug. 14).

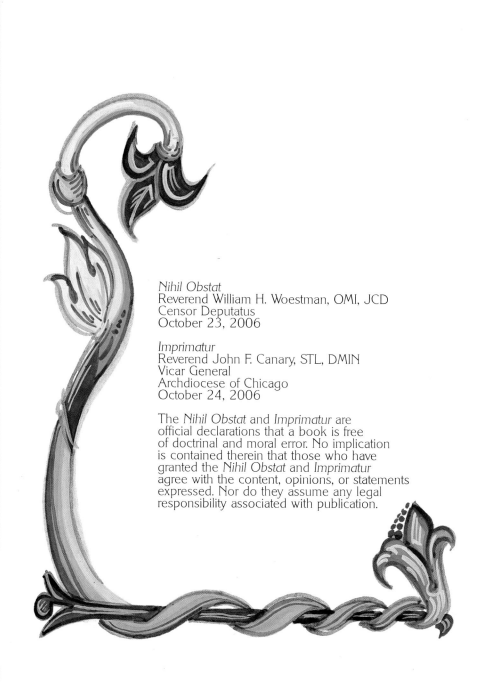

Nihil Obstat
Reverend William H. Woestman, OMI, JCD
Censor Deputatus
October 23, 2006

Imprimatur
Reverend John F. Canary, STL, DMIN
Vicar General
Archdiocese of Chicago
October 24, 2006